Wilderness Years

Poems of Suffering and Transformation

P.M Hill

chipmunkapublishing
the mental health publisher

P.M Hill

All rights reserved, no part of this publication may be reproduced by any means, electronic, mechanical photocopying, documentary, film or in any other format without prior written permission of the publisher.

>Published by
>Chipmunkapublishing
>United Kingdom

http://www.chipmunkapublishing.com

Copyright © P.M Hill   2017

ISBN   978-1-78382-354-3

Wilderness Years

November 2015

Dedicated to the important Ann's in my life

ACJ

AD

AH

P.M Hill

Wilderness Years

5th March 2001

Dear Philip,

Thank you for letting me see your poetry.

I found them most enjoyable, if one can ever describe poetry as enjoyable.

Speaking as one poet to another I thought that 'eulogy for the invisible' was very moving. I thought that it worked particularly well, with the image of something being visible or invisible as the underlying currency on which the movement in the poems was built. I also liked the poem 'retracted affirmation'. It had a good dramatic turn at the end. It is clearly a felt poem, perhaps even a personal poem. But, it works because the feelings have been controlled and put to effective use rather than just exhibited.

I hope you keep writing. It is difficult to know why one writes, or more specifically why I write. Part of it I think is just the sheer delight in the use of words to capture a particular mood or situation. But also that in poetry, the words themselves are the media in which one works. In other words it is not just that one wants to tell a story but that in the telling the most effective words, the most appropriate words and the most euphonic words for the context have been selected and put to good use. The trick us to keep writing, to keep trying different vehicles, different expressions, different metaphors and so on, to accurately tie down an idea.

Very best wishes

Psychiatrist Professor Femi Oyebode Professor of Psychiatry University. Of Birmingham.

P.M Hill

Wilderness Years

The Church of Money

Sat in a pew,
With a service sheet
That looks new,

Click on the switch,
To cure that week long itch,

Sermon through a screen
Six numbers yet to be seen

Flogging their next song
A pop band yearns to belong

Shouting through the microphone
The priest summons the
drawmaster with a drone

Draw machine Lancelot
brought to you by Camelot

Set of balls number three
Lucky for some but is it for me

Good luck everyone the celebrity says
The draw we've waited for seven days

Flashing light the first ball the first
Ball is noted
It previous appearances are then quoted

Checking the service sheet the viewer
kneels
At the coffee table, pen in hand, the
Numbers revealed

The offertory ball is number six
This week he sighs his luck is betwixt

Then the last two balls are drawn

P.M Hill

The viewer lets out a great long yawn

The dismissal is brief as
The fanfare begins
Next weeks services is essential viewing

Dedicated to that gambling teetotaler
Wayne Morris
8th February 2001

Wilderness Years

The meaning of recovery.

Where there is no hope
There is no meaning
You can only find meaning
Through hope

Where there is no affirmation
You can feel invisible
You can only find true love
Through affirmation

Where there is no forgiveness
The power to love diminishes
You can only find forgiveness
Through understanding

Where there is no faith
Doubt has not been overcome
In dealing with doubt
Our faith grows stronger

Where is no grieving
Losses are not acknowledged
You can only find emotional gain
Through emotional pain

Where there is no stigma
Your identity is accepted
You can only deal with prejudice
Through Celebrating your difference.

Dedicated to Fiona Breckenridge – the best friend anyone could have.

January 28th 2001

Eulogy For the Invisible.

Picture This
The first experience of being
A foetus
On a womb photoscan
A divine mission
To be Victim of all
Inhaling its first breath of air
It was visible

Picture this
A boy living in fear
Of mothers raised voice
Of being thrown to the floor
Of playing tidily inside
a 3 foot square hidden barrier
He was invisible

Picture this
A lonely boy
Fourteen years old
with an eight o'clock
curfew
No friends, but bullies
Confiding in his brother
He is invisible

Picture This
A teenage man covered in a blanket
On a street
Asking for change
Escaping his brutal family reality
No dignity in poverty
He drifts away
He is invisible

Picture This
A madman
In a urine scented asylum
No choice of friends
A communion of outcasts

Wilderness Years

No one believes their stories
They are invisible

Picture This
An undiscovered decaying body
No one had missed him
No one had cared
The scrounger had died
He was invisible

Picture This
A crematorium service
35 years summed up in ten minutes
A routine eulogy from the pulpit
In a meat factory for the dead
Half a dozen people looking on
He was invisible

Picture This
Summaries of tragic lives
Removal of their own identities
Labelled as bad or mad and given
Given remedies that seem to take the pain away
Leaving behind tiny corpses inside a huge shells
Chasms of emptiness within
Stigmatised and ignored in crowded rooms
Ultimately rejected
Wasted and futile experiences
It was all suddenly visible

Picture this
An angry outburst
Blessed are those who suffer in vain
And those who are humble and meek
The human punchbags every one of them
They have the Kingdom of heaven
But they believed in life before death too

Dedicated to the Unknown victims of abuse within families

Written between January the 12th and the 27th 2001.

P.M Hill

Away In a Manger (Part Two).

No one could be found as a genuine helper,
No room in the community shelter
No stable but a revolving door,
Three men had visited their assessment according to the law
And his angel had deserted him once more
To a stale smelling asylum
The only shelter
A lonely man slumped on a bed,
That he called his helter skelter,
No visiting this place of living dead
An Aunt called Rene through groceries she sifts
From what she pulled out she bore him gifts,
An apple, a packet of biscuits and a bottle of milk,
A baby he had once also lain, in swaddling sheets,
His boasted second coming they did not greet.
She sat as he cried, his conception was overdue
That as mad as he could be
He could have feelings too
She suspended his hand and it quivered a lot
That's the way it is she said when your nerves are shot
I sat in the church as her eulogy was read
It was not that bad but a great deal went unsaid
And I told my brother the missing plot
Then he said that she told him before she had died
That returning home from the visit she had cried

Dedicated to Rene Somerville 1921- 1995

Written 25th and 26th December 2000

Wilderness Years

MOTHERS EMBRACE

Indoctrinated by her mother,
Abused in an asylum,
She'd watched her kids taken from her,
One by One

Locked away for four years.
Put in a straight jacket in a padded cell,
They stripped her of her own will,
Thought by thought.

Chased through city streets,
Force fed Electro Convulsive Treatment
They destroyed parts of her m emory,,
Recollection by recollection.

Living on city streets,
Sleeping in a cardboard box,
She discovered her own identity,
Year by year,

At 70 years of age
Her first birthday party,
She was given recognition as a human being,
Candle by candle

Stripped of motherhood
Sitting alongside her son
They hugged together expressing what they could not say
Second by second,

Living with cancer,
Avoiding the medics that had abused her,
She finally died in her own way,
Cancellation by cancellation.

Dedicated to the Late Iris Hill by her son Philip Hill.

Written November 2000

P.M Hill

RETRACTED AFFIRMATION

When emphatic smiles greet everything you say,
Your long last emptiness disappears.

When hysterical laughter is a response to all your quips,
Someone finally understands you.

When everything you say seems interesting to her,
Conversations last an hour

When someone beautiful tells you, you're special,
Something unlocks inside

Then you feel your dronings are relevant
Then you feel your intensity is interesting
Then you feel your ugliness is attractive

And when she understands what she means to you,

The smiles turn to frowns
Her gaze avoids you
The conversation stops

Without her I could have
                Lived with my mirror image
                Continued to talk to myself
                Lived with my intensity

But now

                My ugliness is intensified
                My pain is complete.

Wilderness Years

BEFORE GOOD FRIDAY

In a pool of blood the body lay
Inside a porch way door

A simple job
A simple knock
A simple doorcreak
A simple pistol shot
A Catholic ransom paid

someones husband
someones father
someones brother
someones friend
An empty space

A protestant and life
A catholic life
A protestant life
A catholic life
Some Empty spaces

In pool of blood the body lay
Inside a garage door

He finally pictured the friend

> the father
> the brother
> the husband
> for that simple job

And the emptiness had overtaken him

Two victims, one war.

Written October 2000

P.M Hill

POEM FOR WORLD MENTAL HEALTH DAY 2000

when you are hurting so much inside you do not want to go on
you have to forgive

when your so ashamed of yourself that you think your beyond redemption
you have to forgive

when the person you love most in the world rejects and despises you
you have to forgive

when you write to a person for forgiveness and they don't write back
you have to forgive

when your excluded and no one trusts you
you have to forgive

you have to forgive when an ex friend describes you as a problem

you have to forgive when someone you love continues to hurt you

when your mental illness is stigmatised as part of your personality

you have to go on forgiving, forgiving and forgiving again

even when the pain won't go away

even when you can't think straight

even when your still angry with yourself

Then you hope for a time when those feelings of pain, rejection and failure
Don't feel that intense anymore

Wilderness Years

when you can list three things good about yourself

when you can accept a compliment

when you can think about the past without wincing

Its only then that you realise what hard work forgiveness is

Its only then that your forgiven

Written October 2000

P.M Hill

TORTURED GENIUS

I am told I'm a genius
can't take it all in
A meaningless label to
The agonised soul within

I look inside
With the Gospel Phrase
From which I can't hide
That I've
Gained the world
but lost my soul

Searching within I find

I can't forgive myself
For intruding here
Uninvited visits are painful
Outing her fear
and dread of that unexpected April

And I can't live with myself
Wounding the person
I loved most of all
Exterminating that trust
and the fragile link between us

I can't be gentle to that
Fool that I've been
Every encounter with her
Destroys yet more of me within

I can't fast forward from
The skills that I lacked
Wanting to die
But writing another letter instead
And wishing I'd never, never been born

Wanting inspiration
But reading that old story of
That prophet Job

Wilderness Years

and all the time making wishes

Wishing I could forgive
But everything meaningless
Without coming from her

Wishing I could repent
But knowing my limitations
Of journeying onwards

Wishing I could repair
But nothing heals unless
I can put right the pain that I've caused

Wishing I could learn
But knowing that I'm always
On the precipice of further failure

Wanting to better
Could I feel normal again?
Hoping for that letter
With consultants pain
That my pathology could get better?

But I've lost the person I love most
And I fill that hole with everything I can
The tortured genius they say I am

HAPPINESS

I want to be happy
How elusive that is
Everyone so snappy
With no emphasis
On how to copy
Those whose unworldliness
Is philanthropy

I want to be happy
The question I always ask
To those who feel crapy
That underneath our mask
Do we all need therapy?

Can I be happy
Can this be so
Do I sustain psychotherapy
Feelings From which grow
Why I am unhappy

BUILDING ON A ROCK

Unlocking that knotted pain inside
To words of reconciliation that I write
Venting the torrents of feelings I can no longer hide
The unending love continues in spite

Of betrayal, blame and abandonment endured
The fool I am to build on shifting sand
Only in my wife can I feel I am secured
With Unconditional love to an undeserving husband

P.M Hill

DON'T WORRY, BE HAPPY

The tears I've shed for love that
Can't be returned

The hours I've wasted yearning for
What I can't change

The things I've bought to shift
my negative feelings away

From the self loathing, and fear that
consumed me and

All Wasted on the people who don't care
Leaving that
Empty, hollow vacuum inside

Then I think

Build on zero got nothing to lose

Positive thought and action
to each day

Recipricate thought and action
already shown

Give unconditionally and expect
nothing in return

In hope the way I feel will
eventually respond

But I feel

Empty, bitter and twisted inside

Stuck in that grief eternal

Wilderness Years

Pray I no longer wake to face each day

Every distraction returns to grief

So I Learn that

In the middle of the abyss

You plod on and on

In the middle of pain

You smile

In the middle of despair
generate laughter

In the face of futile hope
Always fear to give in

Then after a while you find

Everytime I want to stop
One friend after another tells you, you're wonderful

Everytime I want to quit
The boss tells you that your indispensible

Everytime my book seems at an end
Academics remind the progress I've made

Every single time I want to give in
there is another rason to go on.

In that despair realising:

                forgiveness costs

                a broken heart loves more

P.M Hill

                And Discovering Your humanity

                            Deep Within

Only a God of Love can give me such hope

Dedicated to everyone who calls me a friend

IS LESS MORE?

Revolving round what she thinks
Every encounter another rejection
Circling round those thoughts go round
Nothing to switch them off

Subsiding for a while they go away
Only for them to come back again
Retreating that same brain circuitry again
Thought habit that's difficult to break

Bursting through, a charge of painful impulses
Testing within that limit once more
Reliving what it is to be human again as
The tide flows out once more

Finding the bearings again I replay that footage
Charting my location compass in hand
Is it forwards, backwards or at a station
Thoughts on more than one map

Breaking out of that emotional prison
Departing as a passenger from that long journey
Leaving behind the destination I cannot reach
Setting forth upon my journey to a lesser distance

Choosing who will come with me
Belonging to a small group
But feeling part of a whole
Everything revolving round what they think

Is less more?

8th April 2001

P.M Hill

REDEMPTION SONG

Wearing that troubled look
Rambling in that neurotic monologue
Of self furfilling rejection
Endless recollections of failure
Asking myself what I'm holding for

Wearing that dishevelled jacket
Parading as a fashion victim
The maverick that I am
Is eaten away by pain and grief

Waiting for hope
A wait in vain
You've lost your rights
Conform or your punished
Is there a choice?

Waiting for deliverance
For ten years
From desolate isolation
Friendship from a pariah
Is there a choice?

Waiting for redemption
For the thief that I am
If I defended Christ from my cross
Could I too be saved?
I Steal or Starve
Is that a choice?

Waiting for reconciliation
For the friend that I grieve
If I could switch of those feelings
I pray into my vacuum
Of pain
Or confront that meaningless abyss
Is that a choice?

I wait in the cold and rain
I wait in the snow, I wait in the scorching sun

Wilderness Years

I slept once till one, that day was solved
I walked round the village, that filled an hour
I toyed with jumping into rush hour traffic
and another ten minutes went by

A passer by asks me to move on.
And replying I say

I'm waiting around for a sign of hope
Brought by offers of help
from someone that cares for me
Without that is there a point in going on

I'm waiting for a lifelong friendship
So that one person will always understand me
And I will always feel needed
Without that no one is on my side

I'm marking time for the moment I belong
So that I can tear off my label
And make one I own
Without dignity I am nothing

I'm hanging around anticipating an act of forgiveness
Embodied in a Girocheque
So that I steal no more
Without some money I am condemned

I wait for reconciliation with the friend that I lost
If I wait too long will that matter anymore

I Wish the clock on and on
But each day the same as before
On and on the clock ticks on
Mental Slavery and no end in sight
Do I go on?

P.M Hill

WHO WILL COME TO MY FUNERAL

Who will come to my funeral
I don't care if its big or small
As long as she cares at all

For she is the one I'm angry with
She is the one I love

Draped in flowers the coffin sits
A monument to momentary bliss

But she's not there
She couldn't come
She couldn't face
The deathly scrum
To see the man
She once knew
Under a coffin lid hid from view

Who knew her once
In better days
It had been a craze
To see this man catch her gaze

How he had longed to see once more
But not with that expression at all
Not with gaze that said
I love you no more.

STALKERS ANTHEM

Every breath you take
Every move you make
I'll be watching you

You belong to me
Can't you see

With a love so pure
So suffocating
So raw
The stalker put the pictured of his beloved
In the drawer

To wait for another day
To catch a glimpse
A momentary gaze

Till he could push himself through the
Next phase
Of love unrequited
Rejected Stalled

P.M Hill

MESS UP YOUR HEAD

Don't come near me
I'll mess up your head
To be a friend
To be a neighbour
A help when times are rough
But no closer
Or I'll mess with your head

When love is real
When love is raw

I'll blurt out the score
Then see you no more

Mess with your head
Mess with your head

We are friends no more
We were friends to the end

But now you know the score

We are friends no more.

GET UP STAND UP

Get up stand up
Give the DWP a fight

When moneys tight
Give the DWP a fright
And stand up for your rights

Get up stand up
Robert Nesta Marley sings

To nationwide oppression
To a skewed reality

Of Capita officials
With no humanity
Get up stand up
And alter the reality

Money taken for the nation
My no obligation
To uphold dignity

Get up stand up
Stand up for your right
Against the sanction
Against inaction
And uphold my disability.

Get up stand up
To the decision maker
That I am no faker
And uphold my dignity.

P.M Hill

THE JESUS I KNEW

The Jesus I knew
The Jesus I knew
At School
At Home

Was a friend
That spoke to me

From a time afar
In stories
In classrooms

Across the land

He warned
He scorned

In ways that got to me.
Then and still now

But the Jesus I know now

Is my advocate
And friend

Who loves me
Not so much for who I am

But who I could be
Still with the same warnings
Not from rule books
Or laws on tablets
Not set in stone
Not set in time

But written on my heart
My soul and my DNA

SILVER JUBILEE

God save the Queen
The punk rocker sings

No future in this green and pleasant land.

God save the Queen
Change this regime

No future in this green and pleasant land

God save the Queen
What does she mean
For this green and pleasant land

Send her victorious but omit the second verse

God save the queen

Happy and glorious
Long to reign over us

No future in this green and pleasant land.

P.M Hill

You'll be a man my son

(a hypothetical final poem from father to son).

I told you once you were my son
I told you once that you we're precious
I told you I would never disown you
Or betray you
Whatever you did
Or said or thought
And so it is my son
As I approach the end
I was never discouraged

When you balled at your mum
Mistreated your brother
Or sulked in endless fashion.
Such were your growing pains
Me myself made a man by the army
You yourself graduated to the same height
 you were my son
Even when pupils bullied
and insulted you
when you ran like a coward
when you fell in love
with the idea of
falling in love and had a breakdown
you'll were still my son

I was never disappointed
During that thirty year fog
That chemical straight jacket
I lived to see you
Break those shackles free
To find the real you
And I embraced that
To see the very you
Shine through

But don't implode over my demise

Wilderness Years

you'll still be my son when I am gone
Still I will guide you, Nurture you, Protect you
Love not because of what you do, think or say
I love because you are my mine

There was a time when
Your humanity was under construction
A rite of passage it may have been
but since that re birth
You became a friend and Dwelt within me
just as I did in you

And what's more, You are a man my son.

Philip Hill , Loving Son.

P.M Hill

www.ingramcontent.com/pod-product-compliance
Ingram Content Group UK Ltd.
Pitfield, Milton Keynes, MK11 3LW, UK
UKHW041413180426
11947UKWH00007B/115